NAPOLI. BERGEN.

A CENTURY *of* THE EAST END

The West India Dock Gate, surmounted by a model of the ship *Hibbert*. The gate was demolished in 1932, when the road was widened and the model was taken to Poplar Recreation Ground. After the Second World War an attempt was made to move it to Poplar Library, but the model simply crumbled and had to be scrapped.

A CENTURY *of* THE EAST END

ROSEMARY TAYLOR &
CHRISTOPHER LLOYD

SUTTON PUBLISHING

First published in the United Kingdom in 1999 by
Sutton Publishing Limited · Phoenix Mill
Thrupp · Stroud · Gloucestershire · GL5 2BU

British Library Cataloguing in Publication Data
A catalogue record for this book is available from the British Library.

ISBN 0-7509-2411-X

Front endpaper: Three vessels moored in the Regents Canal Dock, Limehouse *c.* 1920. The three vessels, *Dusty Miller*, *Albion* and SS *Vale* are rigged for display. Normally used at sea for signalling between ships, in port these flags would be rigged for a visiting dignitary, or for a display.
Back endpaper: Panoramic view of the Isle of Dogs, 12 April 1985. In the foreground is Preston's Road, with the two bridges, the entrance into Poplar Dock (now removed) and the Blue Bridge which is the entrance into West India Docks. In the middle is the derelict Canary Wharf, awaiting the grand transformation by the London Docklands Development Corporation. The red brick road, opened by HRH Princess Alexandra in 1983, is just visible.
Half title page: Miss Beatrice Berman, who won the consolation prize at the very first beauty show ever to be held in the East End of London, at the Cambridge Music Hall, Spitalfields, 1904.
Title page: The Beigel Bake in Brick Lane, 1997. The shop is open 24 hours a day, and is a favourite of late-night theatre-goers. It is, in the opinion of many regulars, the best place to get an authentic Jewish beigel (pronounced bygel), and delicious cheesecake.

Typeset in 11/14pt Photina.
Typesetting and origination by
Sutton Publishing Limited.
Printed in Great Britain by
The Bath Press, Bath.

The crest of the London Borough of Tower Hamlets.

Contents

The Great Synagogue in Fournier Street, 1951. Built in 1743 as a chapel for French Huguenots, by 1809 L'Eglise Neuve had been closed and converted into a Methodist chapel, but the dwindling Christian population resulted in it being abandoned in 1895 and by 1897 it was taken over by the Jewish community in Spitalfields and became the Machzike Hadass, the Great Synagogue.

Foreword

I am delighted that you are producing a book celebrating East End life over the past 100 years.

As we look back over the past, the days of poor housing, and the struggle for survival, when a hard day's work at the docks or in a factory was welcomed as an opportunity to earn a few bob to feed the family, when entertainment was an evening at the Troxy or the Regal, or an impromptu street performance, a holiday was a week hop-picking in Kent, and a royal visit was an occasion to bring out the flags and buntings and organise a street party, we realise how impossible it would have been at the beginning of the century to envisage the end.

The East End of London has historically been a place of arrival for immigrants, creating communities of Huguenots, Irish, Jews, Chinese, Somalis and Bengalis, all contributing to the rich cultural mix of the area. The last decade has seen tremendous changes in the East End and with the new developments taking place in the area, such as the regeneration of Banglatown in the Brick Lane area, Canary Wharf rapidly becoming the financial heart of London and the building of the Mile End Millennium Park with its Green Bridge, Tower Hamlets is moving forward into the millennium with every confidence for the future.

Councillor Denise Jones
Mayor of Tower Hamlets

West India Docks, with the Sugar Warehouses in the background, 1920. The warehouses on the north quay were designed by George Gwilt and his son, also George, in 1802, and are considered fine examples of early nineteenth-century dock architecture.

Britain: A Century of Change

Children gathered around an early wireless set in the 1920s. The speed and forms of communication were to change dramatically as the century advanced. (*Barnaby's Picture Library*)

The delirious rejoicing at the news of the Relief of Mafeking, during the Boer War in May 1900, is a colourful historical moment. But, in retrospect, the introduction that year of the first motor bus was rather more important, signalling another major adjustment to town life. In the previous 60 years railway stations, post-and-telegraph offices, police and fire stations, gas works and gasometers, new livestock markets and covered markets, schools, churches, football grounds, hospitals and asylums, water pumping stations and sewerage plants had totally altered the urban scene, as the country's population tripled and over 70 per cent were born in or moved to the towns.

When Queen Victoria died in 1901, she was measured for her coffin by her grandson Kaiser Wilhelm, the London prostitutes put on black mourning and the blinds came down in the villas and terraces spreading out from the old town centres. These centres were reachable by train and tram, by the new bicycles and still newer motor cars, connected by the new telephone, and lit by gas or even electricity. The shops may have been full of British-made cotton and woollen clothing but the grocers and butchers were selling cheap Danish bacon, Argentinian beef, Australasian mutton, tinned or dried fish and fruit from Canada, California and South Africa. Most of these goods were carried in British-built-and-crewed ships, burning Welsh steam coal.

Women working as porters on the Great Western Railway, Paddington, *c.* 1917. (*W.L. Kenning/ Adrian Vaughan Collection*)

As the first decade moved on, the Open Spaces Act meant more parks, bowling greens and cricket pitches. The first state pensions came in, together with higher taxation and death duties. These were raised mostly to pay for the new Dreadnought battleships needed to maintain naval superiority over Germany, and deter them from war. But the deterrent did not work. The First World War transformed the place of women, as they took over many men's jobs. Its other legacies were the war memorials which joined the statues of Victorian worthies in main squares round the land. After 1918 death duties bit even harder and a quarter of England changed hands in a few years.

The multiple shop – the chain store – appeared in the high street: Sainsburys, Maypole, Lipton's, Home & Colonial, the Fifty Shilling Tailor, Burton, Boots, W.H. Smith. The shopper was spoilt for choice, attracted by the brash fascias and advertising hoardings for national brands like Bovril, Pears Soap, and Ovaltine. Many new buildings began to be seen, such as garages, motor showrooms, picture palaces (cinemas), 'palais de dance', and the bow-windowed, pebble-dashed, tile-hung, half-timbered houses that were built as ribbon-development along the roads and new bypasses or on the new estates nudging the green belts.

During the 1920s cars became more reliable and sophisticated as well as commonplace, with developments like the electric self-starter making them easier for women to drive. Who wanted to turn a crank handle in the new short skirt? This was, indeed, the electric age as much as the motor era. Trolley buses, electric trams and trains extended mass transport and electric light replaced gas in the street and the home, which itself was groomed by the vacuum cleaner.

Father and child cycling past Buckingham Palace on VE Day, 8 May 1945. (*Hulton Getty Picture Collection*)

A major jolt to the march onward and upward was administered by the Great Depression of the early 1930s. The older British industries – textiles, shipbuilding, iron, steel, coal – were already under pressure from foreign competition when this worldwide slump arrived, cutting exports by half in two years and producing 3 million unemployed (and still rising) by 1932. Luckily there were new diversions to alleviate the misery. The 'talkies' arrived in the cinemas; more and more radios and gramophones were to be found in people's homes; there were new women's magazines, with fashion, cookery tips and problem pages; football pools; the flying feats of women pilots like Amy Johnson; the Loch Ness Monster; cheap chocolate and the drama of Edward VIII's abdication.

Things were looking up again by 1936 and unemployment was down to 2 million. New light industry was booming in the Home Counties as factories struggled to keep up with the demand for radios, radiograms, cars and electronic goods including the first television sets. The threat from Hitler's Germany meant rearmament, particularly of the airforce, which stimulated aircraft and aero engine firms. If you were lucky and lived in the south, there was good money to be earned. A semi-detached house cost £450, a Morris Cowley £150. People may have smoked like chimneys but life expectancy, since 1918, was up by 15 years while the birth rate had almost halved. The fifty-four hour week was down to forty-eight hours and there were 9 million radio licences by 1939.

In some ways it is the little memories that seem to linger longest from the Second World War: the kerbs painted white to show up in the blackout, the rattle of ack-ack shrapnel on roof tiles, sparrows killed by bomb blast, painting your legs brown and then adding a black seam

A family gathered around their television set in the 1950s. (*Hulton Getty Picture Collection*)

down the back to simulate stockings. The biggest damage, apart from London, was in the south-west (Plymouth, Bristol) and the Midlands (Coventry, Birmingham). Postwar reconstruction was rooted in the Beveridge Report which set out the expectations for the Welfare State. This, together with the nationalisation of the Bank of England, coal, gas, electricity and the railways, formed the programme of the Labour government in 1945. At this time the USA was calling in its debts and Britain was beggared by the war, yet still administering its Empire.

Times were hard in the late 1940s, with rationing even more stringent than during the war. Yet this was, as has been said, 'an innocent and well-behaved era'. The first let-up came in 1951 with the Festival of Britain and then there was another fillip in 1953 from the Coronation, which incidentally gave a huge boost to the spread of TV. By 1954 leisure motoring had been resumed but the Comet – Britain's best hope for taking on the American aviation industry – suffered a series of mysterious crashes. The Suez debacle of 1956 was followed by an acceleration in the withdrawal from Empire, which had begun in 1947 with the Independence of India. Consumerism was truly born with the advent of commercial TV and most homes soon boasted washing machines, fridges, electric irons and fires.

The *Lady Chatterley* obscenity trial in 1960 was something of a straw in the wind for what was to follow in that decade. A collective loss of inhibition seemed to sweep the land, as stately home owners opened up, the Beatles and the Rolling Stones transformed popular music, and retailing, cinema and the theatre were revolutionised. Designers, hairdressers, photographers and models moved into places vacated by an Establishment put to flight by the new breed of satirists spawned by *Beyond the Fringe* and *Private Eye*.

Carnaby Street in the 1960s. (*Barnaby's Picture Collection*)

In the 1970s Britain seems to have suffered a prolonged hangover after the excesses of the previous decade. Ulster, inflation and union troubles were not made up for by entry into the EEC, North Sea Oil, Women's Lib or, indeed, Punk Rock. Mrs Thatcher applied the corrective in the 1980s, as the country moved more and more from its old manufacturing base over to providing services, consulting, advertising, and expertise in the 'invisible' market of high finance or in IT. Britain entertained the world with *Cats, Phantom of the Opera, Four Weddings and a Funeral, The Full Monty, Mr Bean* and the *Teletubbies*.

The post-1945 townscape has seen changes to match those in the worlds of work, entertainment and politics. In 1956 the Clean Air Act served notice on smogs and pea-souper fogs, smuts and blackened buildings, forcing people to stop burning coal and go over to smokeless sources of heat and energy. In the same decade some of the best urban building took place in the 'new towns' like Basildon, Crawley, Stevenage and Harlow. Elsewhere open warfare was declared on slums and what was labelled inadequate, cramped, back-to-back, two-up, two-down, housing. The new 'machine for living in' was a flat in a high-rise block. The architects and planners who promoted these were in league with the traffic engineers, determined to keep the motor car moving whatever the price in multi-storey car parks, meters, traffic wardens and ring roads.

The Millennium Dome at Greenwich, 1999. (*Michael Durnan/Barnaby's Picture Collection*)

The old pollutant, coal smoke, was replaced by petrol and diesel exhaust, and traffic noise. Even in the back garden it was hard to find peace as motor mowers, then leaf blowers and strimmers made themselves heard, and the neighbours let you share their choice of music from their powerful new amplifiers, whether you wanted to or not. Fast food was no longer only a pork pie in a pub or fish-and-chips. There were Indian curry houses, Chinese take-aways and American-style hamburgers, while the drinker could get away from beer in a wine bar. Under the impact of television the big Gaumonts and Odeons closed or were rebuilt as multi-screen cinemas, while the palais de dance gave way to discos and clubs.

From the late 1960s the introduction of listed buildings and conservation areas, together with the growth of preservation societies, put a brake on 'comprehensive redevelopment'. Now the new risk at the end of the 1990s is that town centres may die, as shoppers are attracted to the edge-of-town supermarkets surrounded by parking space, where much more than food and groceries can be bought. The ease of the one-stop shop represents the latest challenge to the good health of our towns. But with care, ingenuity and a determination to keep control of our environment, this challenge can be met.

The East End: An Introduction

The East End of London has played a significant role in the history of London and has had its own unique identity for hundreds of years. The East End has its origins in the Manor of Stepney or Stibenhede, which belonged to the Bishop of London and is mentioned in detail in Domesday Book. The area itself is well defined, its boundaries formed by the City of London to the west, the River Thames to the south and the River Lea on its eastern edge, while to the north Victoria Park forms a natural demarcation from Hackney.

The parish of Stepney was made up of fourteen hamlets, which with sub-divisions rose to twenty-one in later years, these being a collection of fishing and farming communities, covering an area of approximately 8,144 acres. These were the Tower Hamlets, which serviced the Tower of London, providing yeoman to guard the tower. Centuries-old names of Wapping, Ratcliff, Shadwell, Limehouse, Bethnal Green, Bromley, Bow, Mile End Old Town, Poplar, Blackwall, Limehouse, Stepney, Spitalfields, Whitechapel, are all as familiar to us today as they were to Stowe when he wrote his *Survey of London*.

The dawn of the twentieth century marked a transition from the old parish boundaries to the new metropolitan boroughs. The huge increase in population had made the parish of Stepney unwieldy and the area was divided into the metropolitan boroughs of Stepney, Bethnal Green and Poplar with part of it going to Shoreditch.

The population of the East End has been enriched over the years by French Huguenots in the seventeenth century, seeking a haven from persecution, the Irish in the early nineteenth century escaping successive famines and seeking to earn a living in the docks, the German, Polish and Russian Jews, from the mid-nineteenth century to just before the First World War, fleeing the terrible pogroms on the continent, and the Chinese and Indian lascars who worked on ships plying between the Far East and England, and began to settle in the East End during the twentieth century. The Chinese formed a significant community in Limehouse from the 1900s until the mid-1930s, when there was a general move to Soho. Indian seamen, mainly of Bengali origin, began to settle in and around Brick Lane during and after the Second World War, but it was following the troubled times between East and West Pakistan during the late 1960s that increasing numbers of Bangladeshis, mainly from the Sylhet region, arrived in Tower Hamlets.

After the First World War, new housing plans by the London County Council aimed at relieving the overcrowding and density of population resulted in the creation of the Becontree Estate in Barking and Dagenham, where thousands of East End families were rehoused. Stepney also implemented a slum clearance project from the 1930s until halted by the onset of the Second World War. Following the war, which took a heavy toll of property, industry and lives in the East End, there was a marked decline in the population, as many families who were evacuated from the area chose not to return, while many of Jewish origin moved to Essex or north London.

During the twentieth century in particular, large-scale employment in public services helped to ease the crises which developed as a consequence of economic booms and recessions. Manufacturing-based industries, which had thrived in the nineteenth century in many instances declined, with the shift towards serviced-based industries. Besides those who worked in the factories and manufacturing businesses, or as homeworkers in the East End, there were those who earned a livelihood plying their trade through the streets and from door to door, and the street seller was a familiar sight even in the postwar era.

The East End of London has from time immemorial been associated with ships, shipbuilding and ship repairing, but by 1912 this great industry had ceased to exist, although a few ship repairing yards remained. The building of the East India and the West India Docks, the London Docks and St Katharine's, from the 1800s onwards, had resulted in a rapid increase in population. This inevitably led to tensions within the community, as people struggled to earn a livelihood. The docks attracted a large labour force, as there was work to be had with the daily loading and unloading of vessels calling from all parts of the world. However, work was generally of a casual nature, when men had to turn up each morning to await the call-up, hoping to catch the foreman's eye, a chance of a ticket and a day's wages. This system of casual labour was not completely abolished until 1967.

The docks continued to play a vital role in the economy of the area and the country until there was a dramatic change of circumstance on Saturday 7 September 1940, when the Luftwaffe targeted London and the East End bore the brunt of the attacks. The docks were set ablaze and the East End endured months of continuous bombardment. Many tragedies occurred: the greatest of all was the Bethnal Green tube disaster on 3 March 1943, when a stampede at the entrance of the underground station resulted in the deaths of 173 men, women and children. Elsewhere thousands of civilians lost their lives, and hundreds of thousands were made homeless. The destruction of whole streets, reduced to rubble, has often been referred to as 'Hitler's slum clearance'.

A great deal of postwar rebuilding took place under the aegis of the newly formed Greater London Council, and as the pace of rebuilding accelerated, tower blocks began to make an appearance on the landscape. The move from dwellings of one or two rooms and small homes to large blocks of flats changed the face of the East End, but older residents still remember the days when their doors were always open, and they could sit on their front step and chat to passing acquaintances.

The London Government Act of 1963 merged the three boroughs of Stepney, Bethnal Green and Poplar into the London Borough of Tower Hamlets, which began to function from 1965, and the East End took on yet another identity.

A decade later there was a dramatic decline in the fortunes of the East End with the closure of the docks. What had once been the hub of the Empire lay deserted, the warehouses empty and abandoned and the docks strewn with rubbish and overgrown with weeds. The decline seemed terminal, but the potential of docklands as an area for regeneration was evident to the developers, and the Enterprise Zone rose out of the ashes of the derelict docks. The Docklands Light Railway, using the old viaducts of the Blackwall and north Greenwich lines, began to run its distinctive blue and red trains. Billingsgate Market moved into its new premises in 1983 and under the guidance of the London Dockland Development Corporation the landscape was transformed, with Cesar Pelli's impressive Canary Wharf tower on the Isle of Dogs dominating the landscape for miles around.

Despite all the turmoil and change throughout the twentieth century, what has not changed is the spirit of the East Enders. They may not have had much, but they made the most of their lives. Holidays were often a few weeks hop-picking down in Kent, or a day trip to Margate or Southend, and the Country Holiday Fund was a way of saving for these trips. Every royal occasion was cause for celebration: jubilees, coronations, and royal visits all called for the flags and bunting to come out, and street parties were organised in every neighbourhood. The royal family held a special affection for the the East End of London and there have been innumerable visits by royalty during this century, from Queen Alexandra's frequent visits, especially to the Royal London Hospital, Queen Mary's trips to Bethnal Green, George VI and Queen Elizabeth's many wartimes visits, right through to the present day, with the recent visit to docklands by Queen Elizabeth II.

Boundaries may be realigned and administrative districts altered, but to those who live east of the Tower of London, it is their own neighbourhood that is important to them and there is a strong sense of community in each area. The people of Spitalfields have triumphed over what they saw as years of neglect, and the transformation from derelict slums to very desirable residences over the past ten years has been nothing short of a miracle. This, along with the Bethnal Green City Challenge and the Bromley by Bow Community Centre with its state-of-the-art health centre, are object lessons in community development. The Mile End Millennium Park with its Green Bridge spanning the Mile End Road, still in the process of being constructed, is one of the most ambitious projects yet undertaken by Tower Hamlets.

On the financial front, businesses, the newspaper industry and international banks have relocated to Canary Wharf and its adjacent buildings, and the East End is fast becoming the hub of international trade once more. The construction of the Jubilee Line extension through Canary Wharf, making an area once at the mercy of the tides, immediately accessible to all parts of London by the year 2000 marks a fitting finale to a century of tremendous change and development.

Canary Wharf tower, 1991. This view shows the fountain in the square and the north and south colonnade buildings.

East End Edwardians

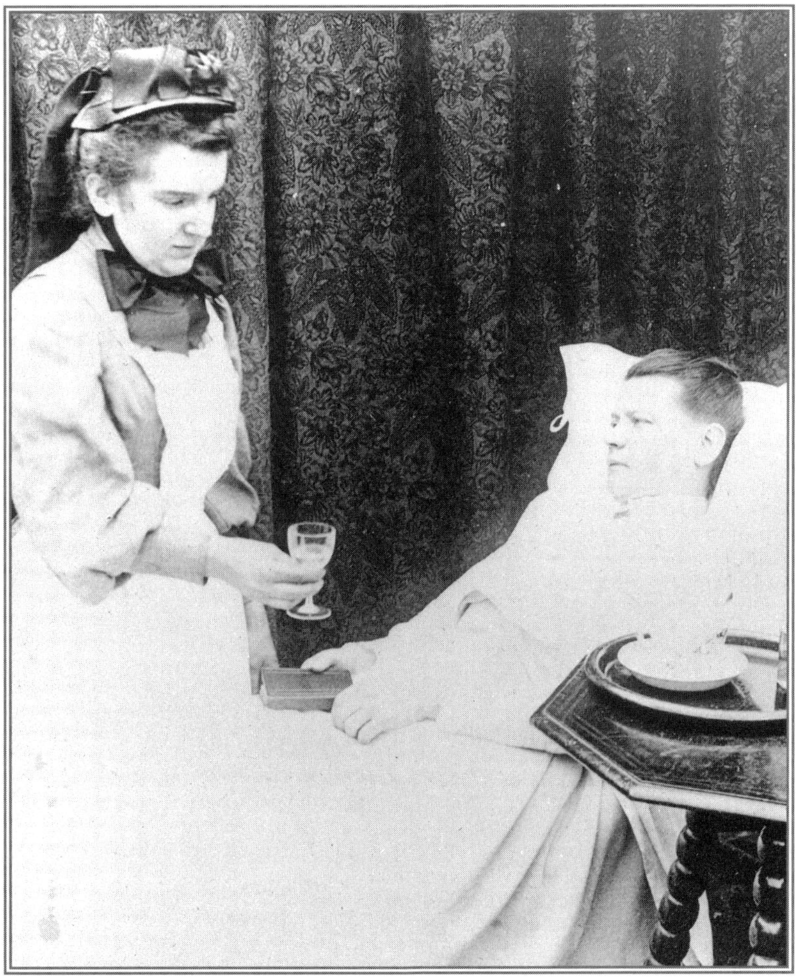

St Mary's Whitechapel, *c.* 1900. A deaconess offers her patient a wineglass of cordial. The scene appears to be 'set up' and was probably one of a set of publicity shots taken by the Revd Cecil Cohen for his fund-raising appeal.

Bow Road underground station, *c.* 1902. The London, Tilbury, Southend & District Railways extension to Barking opened in 1902, and this picture of the newly constructed station was taken shortly afterwards.

A horse bus outside the Mulberry Street public house, 133 Stepney Green, *c.* 1912. The driver of the horse bus is Henry Francis Wiebkin and the farrier by the leading horse is Thomas Ivory. The route was Kew to Liverpool Street, and it is possible that the horse bus travelled the distance in less time than it would take us by car today!

Miss Rose Joseph, the East End's first beauty queen. Rose won the first prize at the very first beauty show to be held in the East End of London, at the Cambridge Music Hall, Spitalfields, 1904. One of the rules of the contest was that the participants were not allowed to improve their appearance by the use of make-up, but had to appear perfectly natural.

Children happily posing for the camera in front of Great Eastern buildings, Quaker Street, *c.* 1914. From the collection of the Revd Cecil Cohen, a curate of St Mary's Whitechapel from 1912 to 1915. The Revd Cohen took a series of photographs of children in the surrounding streets, which he used for his charity appeals.

Queen Alexandra visiting the church of St George's in the East, on the Highway, August 1903. This is possibly the earliest photograph of a royal visit to the East End, although the Queen, who was a patron of the Royal London Hospital, made several visits there later.

The bandstand at Arnold Circus on the Boundary Estate, 1910. The Boundary Estate was one of the major slum clearances of the 1890s, covering an area of around 15 acres, between Virginia Road to the north, Mount Street to the east, Old Nichol Street to the south and Boundary Street to the west. By 1880 the Old Nichol had become one of the most notorious slums in the East End. The population of 5,700 inhabitants were mainly from the criminal elements, and street fights between rival gangs were a regular occurrence. In 1889 the death rate was 40 per 1,000, twice that of the parish of Bethnal Green. Following an Act of Parliament in 1890 for Housing for the Working Classes, the LCC decided to clear the area, demolishing all the houses and building blocks of flats. Arnold Circus, with streets radiating outwards, was created (see p. 104).

A passage in Ratcliff on a wet day, at the turn of the century. The only means of access was by an arched passage about 2 ft wide under one of the houses in the main street.

'Are yer comin' dahn the Lane?' Petticoat Lane on Sunday morning, *c.* 1905. This postcard was produced by Woolf Stationers, Middlesex Street, the official name for Petticoat Lane. The market here has been a traditional place for Sunday morning shopping, and has become a great tourist attraction.

The Russian Vapour Baths, Schevziks, Brick Lane, *c.* 1910. These Jewish baths were situated just opposite the Machzike Hadaass, Great Synagogue, on the corner of Fournier Street and Brick Lane, and were famous in their day. Run by Rabbi Benjamin Schevzik, the Friday afternoon visit by orthodox Jews was part of an East End tradition which continued right up to the beginning of the Second World War. The baths were closed after a fire damaged the interior.

Unveiling of the anchor from the royal yacht *Victoria and Albert* in Poplar Recreation Grounds, July 1911. The little girls in their summer finery are in sharp contrast to the dignitaries in their suits. The anchor was placed on a plinth surrounded by a flowerbed. It was removed during the Second World War, presumably for scrap.

Lord Swaythling, better known as Sir Samuel Montagu MP (1832–1911), *c.* 1900. Born into a Jewish family in Liverpool, Samuel Montagu came to London at the age of 21 and joined the banking profession, becoming the head of a firm of exchange and bullion brokers. In 1885 he was elected MP for Whitechapel. He was created a baronet in 1894 and in 1907 he became a peer. He was well known in the East End for his charity and benevolence among the Jewish people.

Dr Thomas Barnardo, founder of the Ragged Schools in Limehouse, *c.* 1900. Barnardo founded his East End Juvenile Mission in 1868 in Hope Place, Stepney, and in 1870 rented a house at 18 Stepney Causeway, as a lodging house for children. A sign above the doorway read: 'No destitute boy or girl ever refused admission.' He went on to open schools and homes for children, and laid the foundation of one of the largest organisations for abandoned and orphaned children, Dr Barnardo's Homes.

Family portrait from the Tuffel family collection, *c.* 1910. The picture was taken in the Grand Studio at 136 Whitechapel Road. The photographers, Polsky Brothers, opened for business in 1905.

Outram's Dining Rooms, 509 Hackney Road, *c.* 1910. The proprietor Mr Henry Outram and his wife pose in the doorway with members of staff.

The Old Ford Picture Palace, 55 St Stephen's Road, *c.* 1912. Renamed the Ritz after the Second World War, it finally closed in 1961. The proprietor Mr McDonell is standing on the left. The film advertised in the poster by the commissionaire on the right, *Making a Man of Him* was released in 1912.

The First World War

The silent enemy – a naval airship of the Beta type cruising over Cotton Street on the evening of Wednesday 20 October 1915. William Whiffin probably took this photograph from his studio window, which was in East India Dock Road.

Army Recruiting Office, East India Dock Road, 1914. It was adjacent to Poplar Recreation Grounds. The caption on the bus reads 'To Berlin and back free'.

Crisp Street, Poplar, during the rioting which took place after the sinking of the *Lusitania*, May 1915. The crowd is seen here attacking Adolf Schoenfeld's tobacconist's shop. Minutes later, the shop was wrecked and goods and even furniture was carried away, including a harmonium, which was passed down to the crowd from an upstairs window. Many other East End shops were also destroyed and looted during this upsurge of anti-German feeling.

Isaac Rosenberg, poet and painter, with his brother Elkon standing beside him, September 1917. Isaac and Elkon were on leave in London at the time. Isaac Rosenberg's talent was spotted while he was still at school, and he went on to study painting at the Slade School of Fine Art, while continuing to write poetry. Tragically, he was killed in action on 1 April 1918.

Interior of the Upper North Street School, Poplar, June 1917, after the destruction of the classroom when the school was bombed on Wednesday 13 June during a raid by Gotha aircraft. The school was situated in the grounds of what is now a park adjacent to Trinity Church, and the site is marked by a willow tree. The school was one of the many founded in Poplar by George Green. It was later rebuilt a short distance away, and is now called Mayflower School.

The funeral procession of the 18 children killed at the Upper North Street School on 13 June 1917. The cortège is seen passing along East India Dock Road by Poplar station. All the children were buried in a mass grave in East London cemetery, with the exception of two Catholic children who were buried in St Patrick's cemetery, Leytonstone.

The unveiling of the memorial to the children killed in the raid. The statue was unveiled in Poplar Recreation Grounds, East India Dock Road, 23 June 1919.

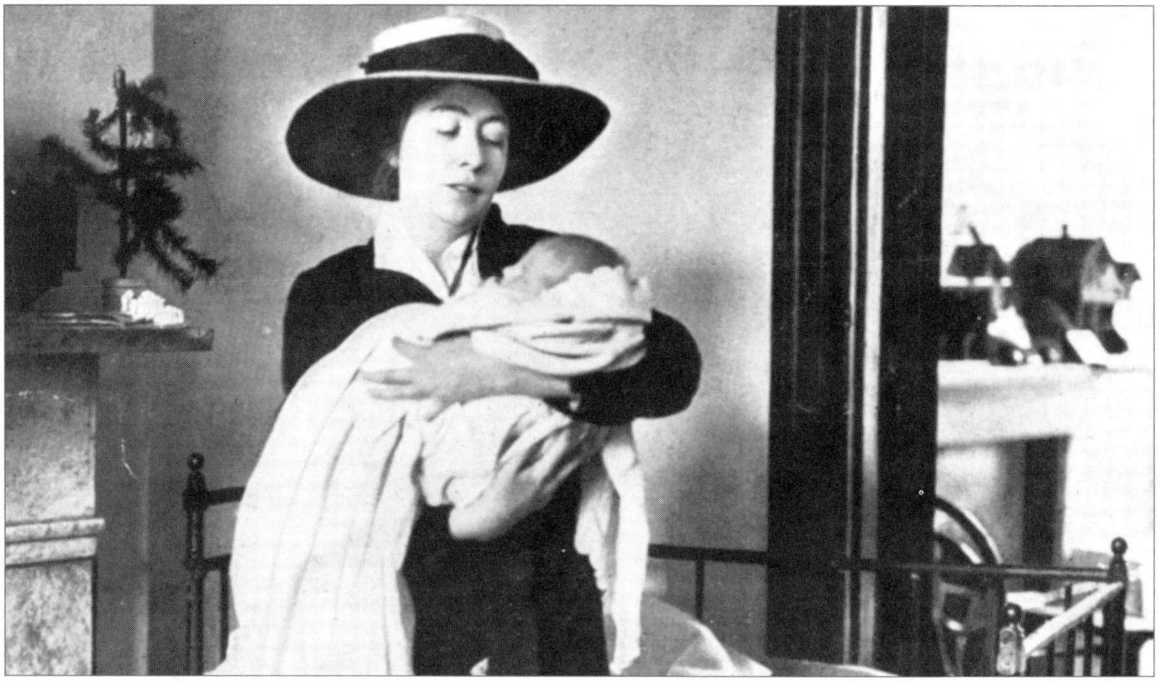

Sylvia Pankhurst with one of the babies at the Mother's Arms, Old Ford Road, 1915. Sylvia Pankhurst came to Bow in 1912, to publicise the cause of women's suffrage. She stayed on to support women and children who suffered as a result of their menfolk being sent away to fight. Among her many schemes to alleviate the distress and hardship brought to these families was the opening of a Mother and Baby Clinic and Nursery in an old pub on the corner of Old Ford Road and St Stephen's Road, called the Gunmaker's Arms, which she and her friends refurbished and renamed the Mother's Arms.

Wounded Belgian soldiers in the Annie Zunz Ward of the London Hospital, 1914. The Belgian connection is particularly poignant here, as it recalls the sacrifice made by Nurse Edith Cavell, who trained and worked at the London Hospital, and was later shot by a German firing squad on 12 October 1915, having been accused of spying in Belgium.

Festival of Children in Victoria Park, August 1916. A group of 60 children from Bow took part in the pageant organised by Sylvia John Bailey, who was Sylvia Pankhurst's cousin, for the East London Federation of the Suffragettes. When the event was advertised, hundreds of children turned up at the Women's Hall, 400 Old Ford Road, for rehearsals and Joan Bailey patiently coached the children, selecting 60 of the best dancers. She dressed them in fine white muslin, with garlands of flowers; the flimsy fabric, however, couldn't disguise the multi-coloured, patched and worn undergarments many of the children wore!

Peace Party in Norman Road, Bow, 1919. The party was organised by Mrs Savoy to mark the Armistice and the end of the Great War. Sylvia Pankhurst and Norah Smythe had set up the East London Toy Factory, a boot factory and a creche at No. 45 Norman Road, seen in the distance to the left of the picture. Mrs Savoy, who died shortly after the war, was a brushmaker by trade and a good friend to both Sylvia Pankhurst and her neighbour George Lansbury, former MP for Bow and Poplar, who championed the cause of Women's Rights.

Will Crooks, MP for North Woolwich, and Sir Alfred Yeo, MP for Poplar, seeing off mothers and children leaving Poplar for a country holiday, outside the Town Hall, Newby Place, July 1917. The mothers had lost children in the Upper North Street School bombing on 13 June 1917.

Old English Fair, Poplar Recreation Ground, August 1919. The fair was an opportunity for the people to celebrate the end of the First World War, and what they believed was lasting peace. It was not only the children who were determined to enjoy themselves – the mayor, councillors and even the local MP took their turn on the rides!

Councillor C.R. Attlee, Mayor of Stepney, 1919. Clement Attlee came to the East End to undertake voluntary work at Toynbee Hall. He entered politics as a councillor in Stepney and was mayor from 1919 to 1920. He was later elected MP for Limehouse, and was Labour's first post Second World War prime minister.

The Mayor of Poplar, the Revd William Lax, at the opening of the Old English Fair, August 1919. The Revd Lax was the flamboyant minister of the Poplar Methodist Church in Woodstock Terrace. He was known for preaching sermons at the dock gates, and counted himself a failure if his sermon lasted less than an hour!

The Mayor of Poplar, Councillor A.H. Warren JP, during a visit to the Mudfield allotments, Millwall, 1918. Two hundred and twenty-four allotments were staked out on ground belonging to the Port of London Authority. The man in the chauffeur's uniform is E.S. Bossley.

Girls dancing in the open air, Poplar Recreation Ground, June 1919. This was one of the many parties held to celebrate the end of the First World War.

New Labour, New Hope

Puppies for sale in Club Row, *c.* 1925. The street, which was just off Bethnal Green Road, north side, was established as a bird and animal fair by the 1850s, with trade spilling over to Sclater Street. It was well-known locally as a place for buying and selling small animals, including stolen dogs! The man pictured here seems to be viewing the cameraman with some suspicion.

Pereira Street, Bethnal Green, 1920. This view of the back yards of Pereira Street was taken from 9 Holmes Avenue (formerly New Square) and is evocative of so many of the cottages which were homes to East End residents. The street ran parallel to Brady Street, and joined Bath Street to the south.

Electric House, Bow Road, corner of Alfred Street was built at a cost of approximately £31,000 and opened on 29 May 1925. The Minnie Lansbury memorial clock and plaque are in place. Minnie Lansbury was the wife of Edgar Lansbury, eldest son of George Lansbury. She worked with Sylvia Pankhurst during the Suffragette Movement, and was an alderman of Poplar during the Poplar Rates Dispute. She was one of five women sent to Holloway in September 1921. She died of pneumonia on 1 January 1922, and was honoured for her heroism with this memorial.

Floods in Wapping High Street, probably in 1928, when there was devastating flooding all along the Thames. Rescue teams were kept busy rescuing hundreds of residents trapped in their homes.

Pearly Kings and Queens in procession in the East India Dock Road, 1920s. The Pearlies regularly helped to raise funds for the Poplar Hospital. In the distance can be seen the East India Dock entrance gate with its distinctive clock tower.

Dock employees at no. 10 and Eastern Dock Dept, London Dock, pictured on 10 May 1920 by H.S.G. Grant, photographer. Those seen here include A.J. Hone, N. Smith, G. Armitage, W.G. Onbridge. F. Wolton, A. Dickenson, C.E.P. Harbat, E.S. Tooth, H.W. Daniel, A. Howard, V. Walker and E. Smith.

Outside Poplar Town Hall, Newby Place, September 1921. The people come out to hear George Lansbury and the councillors make their speeches before they are marched off to Brixton and Holloway. In 1919 Lansbury and the Labour councillors of Poplar decided to make a stand against the high rates levied by the council, in order to pay for out-relief to poor families, among other things. Their refusal to levy rates, despite threats from the government, eventually resulted in the conviction and imprisonment of thirty councillors. However, they did achieve their aim of the equalisation of rates across London, and the term 'Poplarism' entered the language.

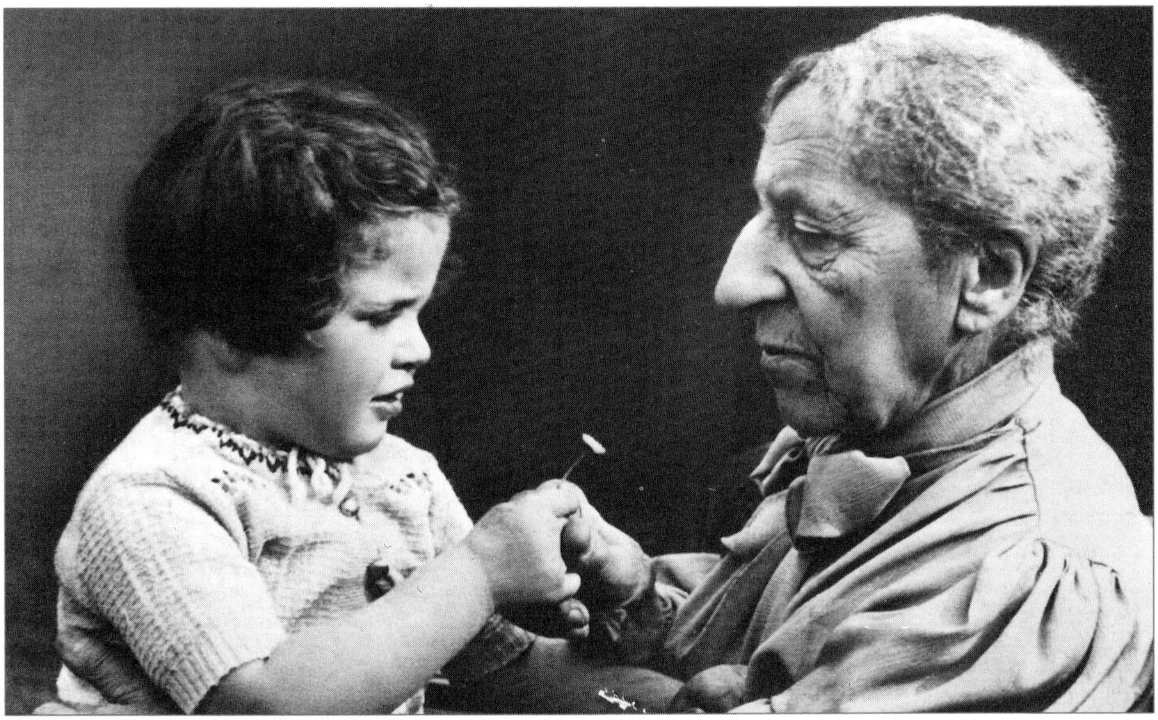

Alice Model (1856–1943) and one of her small charges, *c.* 1925. Alice Model was a pioneer in the nursery and health care service for the Jewish community in the East End. In 1896 she started a Jewish day nursery, and in the 1920s founded the Jewish Maternity Hospital in Underwood Street in Whitechapel.

Boys and girls from the Stepney Jewish Clubs, 1929. Some of the children look rather bemused at having their picture taken. There was a large Jewish population in Stepney and Bethnal Green during the early years of the century up to the Second World War, and clubs were opened to cater for the needs of Jewish children.

The Duchess of York, later Queen Elizabeth, opens the Docklands Settlement, 30 April 1924. She is accompanied by the sub-warden in charge, Mr H.W. Kimberley, as young Docklands children look on in awe.

The Duke and Duchess of York arriving at the Docklands Settlement, 30 April 1924. This was one of their very first engagements after their marriage. Here the Duke and Duchess are welcomed by Mr R. Kennedy-Cox.

Three West Indian seafarers outside the Strangers Home, West India Dock Road, 1926. Seafarers from all nations came to the Strangers Home in search of lodgings. The Home for Asiatics, Africans and South Sea Islanders was opened in June 1857, to serve the needs of foreign seamen or lascars, who were often recruited to crew ships from the Far East, only to be discharged and left to fend for themselves in the streets of the East End. It closed in the 1930s, and was demolished during Stepney's rebuilding programme.

George Lansbury, Mayor of Poplar, cutting the first sod on the Chapel House Street estate, Isle of Dogs, 13 January 1920. Others in the group include Cllr J.J. Rugless, Sir Alfred Yeo (with pipe), J.B. Skeggs, Town Clerk, Cllr A. Baker and Harley Heckford, Borough Surveyor and Engineer.

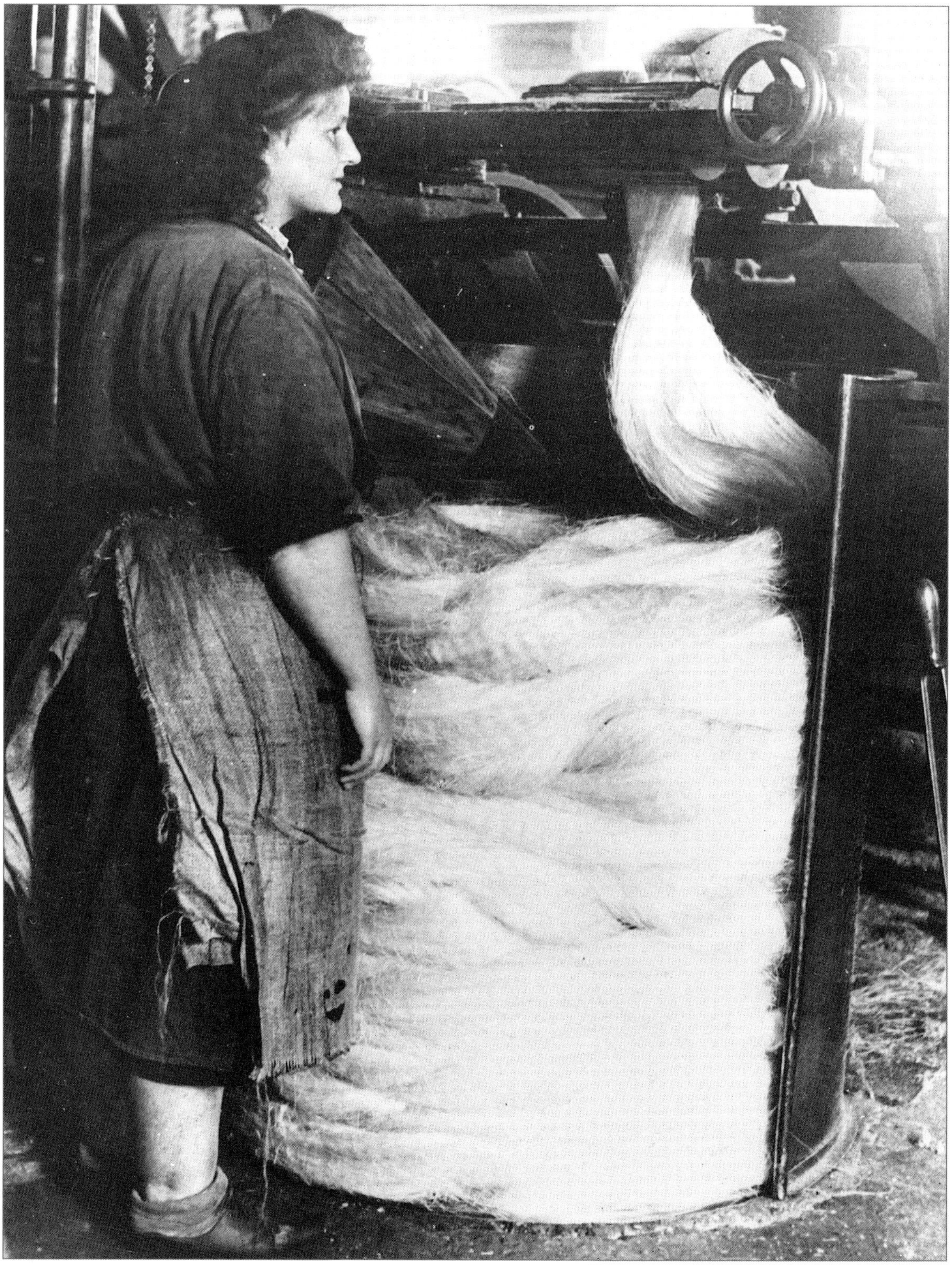

A young woman worker minding the machine at Hawkins & Tipson's Globe Rope Works, Millwall, on the Isle of Dogs, 1920s. Rope was made from hemp or manilla fibre, which was spun and twisted into strands of varying thickness. The Globe Rope Works opened in 1881 and closed in 1971.

Floods at Orchard Place with a rescue operation in progress, 7 January 1928. A young lady is being helped out of a boat and pulled up over the parapet. The flooding, the result of a tidal surge, devastated much of the Isle of Dogs and surrounding areas, and resulted in the relocation of the entire community in the Leamouth area by the early 1930s. The Thames Barrier, completed in 1982, now prevents such incidences from recurring.

Staff and workers of the East London Toy Factory in the garden of 45 Norman Road, 1920s. The toy factory was set up in October 1914 by Sylvia Pankhurst and Norah Smyth, of the East London Federation of the Suffragettes, to provide work for women and girls, especially those with babies and young children, who often found it difficult to work long factory hours. The toy factory moved from Bow to King's Cross in 1936–7.

General Strike, 1926. Strikers are seen here stopping a petrol lorry in East India Dock Road, by Bow Lane. The General Strike, which began at midnight on 3 May and ended nine days later at noon on 12 May, was a result of the failure of miners and mine owners to come to an agreement on the proposed reduction in wages and increased working hours. The TUC supported the miners by calling for a national strike.

Troops passing along East India Dock Road during the General Strike, 1926. The government was determined that loading and unloading of merchandise in the docks continued uninterrupted and Winston Churchill, Chancellor of the Exchequer, pressed for a militant response to the strikers. The strike was one of the bitterest in the East End, but ultimately it was a failure.

The Duchess of York waving to the crowds at the opening of York Hall, 1929. The Duke and Duchess of York opened the new public baths and wash-houses in Old Ford Road, Bethnal Green, which were later named York Hall.

Teddy Baldock, World, British and European Bantamweight Champion, 1927. Starting out his boxing career at Premierland in Backchurch Lane off Commercial Road, Baldock fought on to become bantamweight champion of the world in 1927 at the age of 19, when he beat Archie Bell in a 15-round contest at the Albert Hall.

The Duke and Duchess of York with the Mayor, Cllr W.C. Chandler JP, the mayoress and councillors on the steps of York Hall, 5 November 1929. The Duchess of York wears a demure smile for the camera, but the Duke appears to be making a comment to Mrs Chandler, who is doing her best to remain serious.

J.C. Riddell, T. Chivers and John Bussey JP, three veteran members of the Poplar Benevolent Society, 1923.

Queen Mary touring Bethnal Green on foot, 5 May 1928. In attendance is the Mayor of Bethnal Green, Mr M.H. Seymour. The Queen came to Bethnal Green to attend a performance of *Il Pagliacci* by the Oxford House Choral Society. She alighted from her car in Mansford Street and walked through the streets. The Queen spent two hours in the Excelsior cinema and then proceeded to Oxford House.

Always Something to Celebrate

Alderman John Scurr and Councillor Julia Scurr, 1921. John and Julia Scurr were married in 1900 and were involved in political activities all their married life. Elected to the Poplar Council in 1919, they were both involved with the Poplar Rates Dispute and were imprisoned along with the other councillors in September 1921. John Scurr was elected as MP for Mile End in 1923. He died in 1932 and is commemorated by John Scurr House in Branch Road and John Scurr School in Cephas Street. Julia Scurr was a member of the Board of Guardians and was an active suffragette, leading delegations of women workers to Downing Street to press for improvements in the working conditions of East End women. She died in 1927, and despite her prominent political career has not been honoured.

Three Burmese seafarers in a café on the Burmese Trading Company premises, West India Dock Road, 1932. Lascars were a common sight in the streets around Poplar in the first half of this century. The shipping companies found it convenient to hire lascars, who were paid a fraction of the wage given to seafarers of British origin, and they would be paid off after the voyage and left to arrange their own return passage.

Regents Canal Dock, Limehouse, 1930. A busy scene of ships and barges, recalling the heyday of docklands, when the Port of London was the largest and busiest in the world.

No. 42 bus in Cambridge Heath Road, Bethnal Green, 1937. The bus is passing no. 242, which has a coronation banner displaying the words 'Long Live the King'. Behind the bus is D.J. Leman Ltd, cardboard box manufacturers. The no. 42 route was from Amhurst Road in Hackney to Camberwell Green.

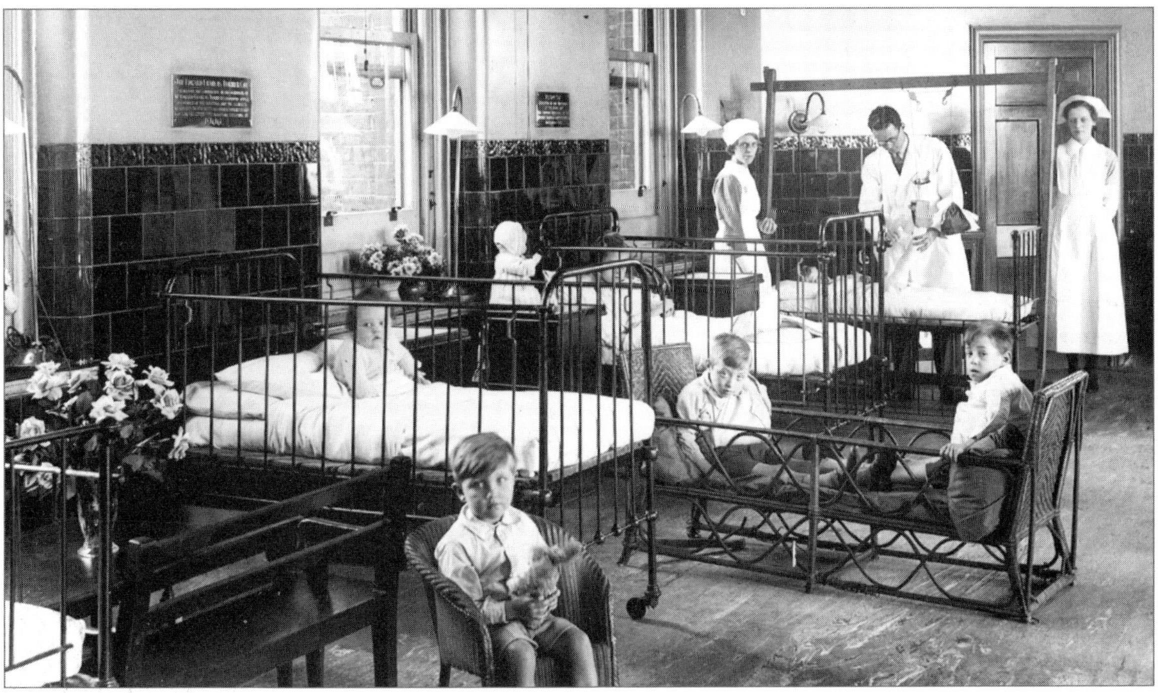

The Edward Francis Turner cot in the Children's Ward at Poplar Hospital, 1930s. Built in the 1850s when it became clear that there was a great need for a hospital in the vicinity of the docks, it was originally for emergencies only. The hospital was badly damaged during the Second World War, and was later closed and demolished.

The Troxy cinema opens in Commercial Road, Stepney, with the British première of the film *King Kong*, 1933. The Troxy was converted in 1963 into the London Opera Centre, a training school for young opera singers and coaches, and more recently into a bingo hall. Times have certainly changed!

Interior of the Troxy, 1933. This view shows the opulent fittings and décor which rivalled that of the Rivoli in Whitechapel.

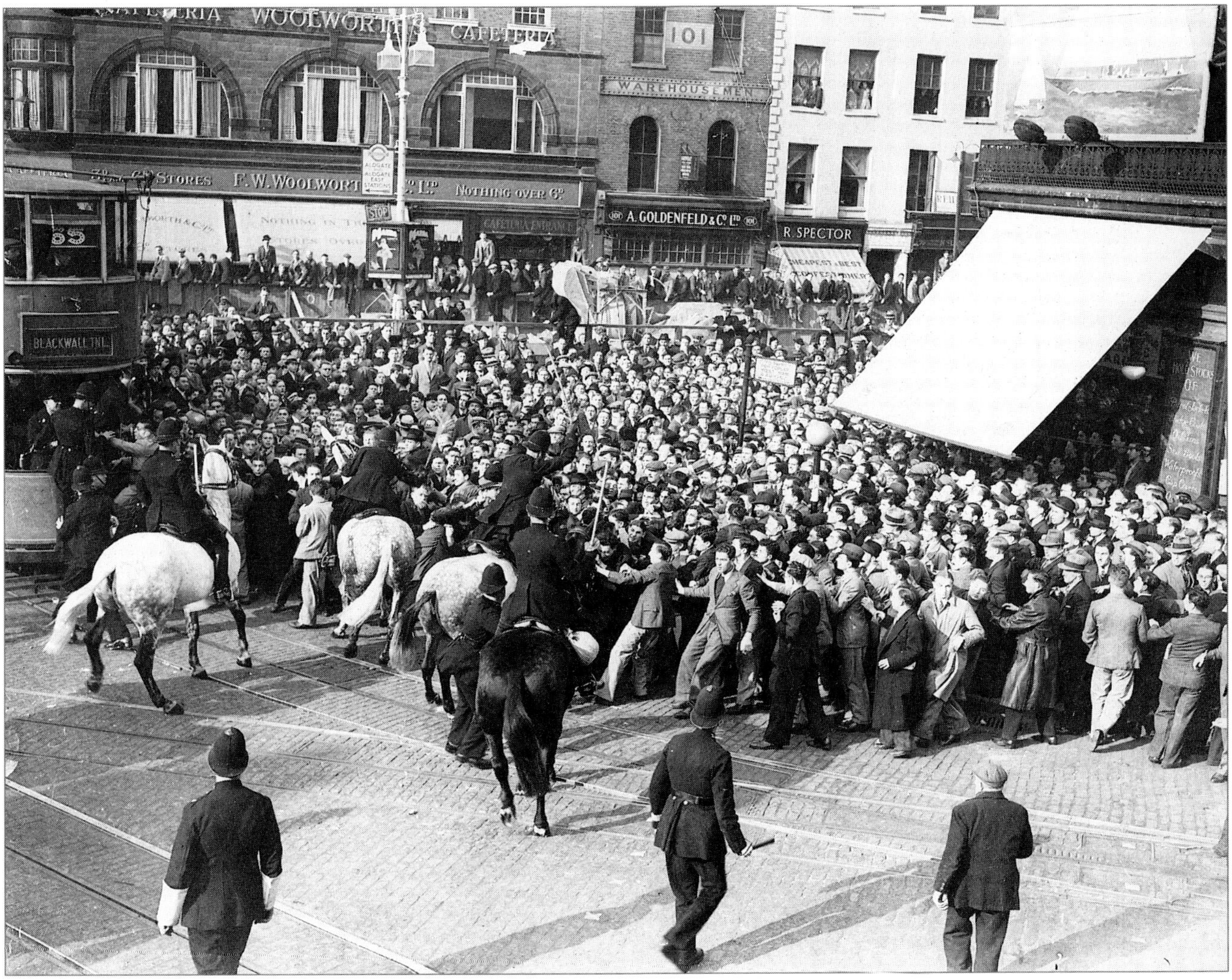

Before the Battle of Cable Street, 4 October 1936. Half an hour before Sir Oswald Mosley's Blackshirt procession through the East End of London was due to start, the crowds at Gardiner's Corner had blocked the route, and mounted police with batons force their way through. Despite the efforts of the police force, the combined strength of the Irish dockers and the Jewish community succeeded in halting the fascist march. The Woolworth store in the background was on the corner of Whitechapel High Street and Commercial Street. On the extreme left is the no. 65 tram from Whitechapel to the Blackwall Tunnel.

A Chinese restaurant proprietor chooses his meat for the menu, 1932. The Low Hong Kong Dining Rooms were at 60 Pennyfields, Limehouse, where there was a considerable Chinese community. Live chickens are being examined and selected for the evening meal.

Two women and the local greengrocer exchange pleasantries in Salter Street, Limehouse. This picture was taken on 4 November 1932, although the women don't look as if they are dressed for the cold weather.

A special appearance at the newly opened Rivoli Theatre by Sophie Tucker, the American jazz singer. The theatre was opened on Monday 1 August 1921, on the site of the old Wonderland, and was considered to be the last word in luxury. During its first week the programme included W.S. Hart in *Sand*, *The Mutiny of Elsinore*, *A Yankee at the Court of King Arthur* and *Carmen*.

George V and Queen Mary during their visit to Limehouse Town Hall, 25 May 1935. A fine view of the procession with the carriage carrying the King and Queen to the Town Hall in Commercial Road where they met the mayors of the three East London Boroughs.

Queen Mary with Brigadier General Sir Wyndham Deedes, visiting gardens in Bethnal Green, 1935. Sir Wyndham Henry Deedes lived at Temple House, 17 Victoria Park Square, from 1923 to 1939, following a distinguished career in the army intelligence service in Cairo and Palestine. He retired to Bethnal Green and served on the council and the LCC.

Tram and general traffic in the Mile End Road, on a foggy day in November 1933. In the background is Wickhams department store.

Mrs Biggs, wearing a crown, serves refreshments from her front room in Giraud Street, Poplar, during the coronation celebrations, 1937. The East End held street parties and celebrations and decorated their houses and shops in honour of King George VI and Queen Elizabeth.

Mothers leaving the council offices, High Street, Poplar, with perambulators presented by the mayor, Cllr Adams, to the ten babies born on Jubilee Day, 6 May 1935.

A view of the newly built cottages at Malam Gardens, the Commercial Gas Company estate in the East India Dock Road, when they were completed in 1935. The development was named after John Malam, who was a pioneer in gas meter design.

Eagle House, Poplar High Street, after being converted into self-contained flats, 1933. The picture shows the back of what was once the Eagle Tavern.

Prince Ras Monolulu, probably the best-known racing tipster of the time in England, seen in action in Club Row, 1936. Prince Monolulu paraded the streets around Petticoat Lane dressed in baggy trousers and a flamboyant head-dress of ostrich feathers, calling out, 'I gotta horse'. While many thought him an African prince, he was in fact a Maori, Peter McKay, who came to England at the turn of the century. He died in his late eighties, in 1965.

George Lansbury and John Silley, of Messrs Green & Silley Weir, ship repairers of Blackwall, playing bowls on the lawn of Jubilee Crescent, the home of 300 retired shipwrights at Cubitt Town, during a garden party in July 1938.

The first ARP class in Poplar, inaugurated on 25 April 1938. This picture shows the first woman warden to receive her badge. The clouds gather.

The East End Blitzed

Queen Elizabeth visits the Brady Street site, 17 June 1943. Iris Madle, two years old, has just presented the Queen with a bouquet of carnations. Mr Ellis is next to the Queen, and the Mayor, Cllr Tate and the Town Clerk are in the rear.

Rip the ARP dog was found by Warden E. King of Post B 132 during the blitz of 1940. Adopted by the wardens' post in Southill Street, Rip helped to find trapped people and was the first dog on this type of job. He was awarded the Blue Cross Medal of the Dumb Friends League. The medal was instituted by Maria Dickin, founder of the People's Dispensary for Sick Animals, and referred to as 'the animals' VC'.

Rip surveys the damage after a heavy night of bombing in Poplar, 27 July 1941. Wardens of Post B 132 helped to dig out casualties caused by a parachute mine. The scene is at the junction of Arcadia Street and Latham Street.

ARP workers and wardens attached to Post B 132 have the unpleasant task of helping to dig out people killed in these Poplar dwellings as the result of blast from a parachute mine, 27 July 1941.

Bomb damage to Columbia buildings and Columbia Market, 1943. Columbia Market and the surrounding dwellings were the gift of Baroness Angela Burdett-Coutts, Victorian heiress and philanthropist, who spent a great deal of her fortune attempting to alleviate the poverty she saw in the East End. The market was eventually demolished in 1962.

Mrs Roosevelt, wife of the United States' President, visited the Tilbury shelter with King George VI in October 1942. The shelter was in the warehouse of the London, Tilbury, Southend & District Railway in Alie Street, Stepney, and there are stories of how people broke into the warehouse to shelter there during the worst days of the blitz.

Warship Week 21–8 March 1942. A large banner is displayed outside the Bethnal Green Town Hall in Cambridge Heath Road urging people to donate towards the fund for the war effort. Bethnal Green had several of these fund-raising campaigns.

Workmen fixing handrails in the tube shelter entrance following the tragic incident on 3 March 1943, when 173 men, women and children lost their lives during a stampede down the poorly-lit stairs at the entrance to Bethnal Green underground station, which was one of the area's main designated air raid shelters. This incident was the worst civilian disaster to have taken place during the Second World War.

The Revd H.R. Peerless in his ruined church, St Simon Zelotes, Bethnal Green, following an air raid on 21 October 1943.

Queen Elizabeth visiting the Sewardstone Road piggery, 17 June 1943. The mayor and post warden J. Shepherd are in attendance, and while Her Majesty shows a keen interest in the porker, the mayoress looks less than enthusiastic.

Children in Bethnal Green, 1943. Many of these children have had their homes bombed, but have cleared away the bomb damage and made allotments which they looked after themselves. Reg, seen from behind, was a member of the committee formed to organise the children, who watched the allotments all through the day.

Children in Bethnal Green, 1943. The scene is in Russia Lane, near Bishops Way, where the children are seen clearing a new site for an allotment. The children were trying to help the people by growing food such as peas, potatoes and cabbages, using gardening tools borrowed from the fire brigade.

War Weapons Week 17–24 May 1941. The young lads pictured here are obviously fascinated by the artillery on display at an exhibition in the Central Library lecture hall, Bethnal Green.

Warship Week, 21–8 March 1942. The 'Bee-Gees' Concert Party helping to raise funds at the Bethnal Green Town Hall, Patriot Square and obviously having a good time as well. These 'Bee-Gees' obviously pre-date the Gibb brothers pop group by some twenty years!

Stein's clothiers, demolished in an air raid on 10/11 May 1941. Stein's was on the corner of Club Row and Bethnal Green Road. This bleak scene is just one of many photographs in the Tower Hamlets Local History Collection of the devastation caused by Hitler's bombs.

The first V1 flying bomb to fall in London landed in Grove Road on 13 June 1944. The bomb fell on the corner of Grove Road and Antill Road, and there is now a plaque on the railway bridge across Grove Road, commemorating this event.

Warship Week in Bethnal Green, 21–8 March 1942. Electricity Department display truck at the Digby Street Depot. The banner on the truck urges people to invest in War Savings Certificates.

The Bethnal Green Electricity Department attends a call at Whitman House, on the Cornwall Estate, during the early years of the Second World War.

King George and Queen Elizabeth, accompanied by the Princesses Elizabeth and Margaret in Bethnal Green, 9 May 1945. The royal family are on a VE Day plus one victory visit to the East End.

Peace parade in Cambridge Heath Road, Bethnal Green, 7 June 1946. Tanks rumble through the streets in celebration of the end of the war.

Picking up the Pieces

Christmas in Bethnal Green, 1952. The Mayor and Mayoress, along with the Vicar of St John's Church, the Revd O'Brien Hamilton, watch a little girl picking her gift from Santa's sack.

Opening of the Odeon cinema, Cambridge Heath Road, Bethnal Green, 10 October 1949. Dirk Bogarde is seen in conversation with the Mayor Cllr Tate, and his daughter, the Mayoress. The Odeon was previously the Foresters, a music hall.

Hooke House, Thoydon Road, 1950. Built to accommodate 48 families, the block was named after Alderman H. Hooke, then chairman of Bethnal Green's Housing Committee. A large crowd gathers to watch the laying of the foundation stone, and have a ready smile for the cameraman.

The first tenant moves into the new Lansbury Estate, Gladstone House, Poplar, 14 February 1951. Mr and Mrs Albert Lloyd Snoddy, their two children and Mrs Snoddy's mother moved into a four-room ground floor flat in the first block to be completed by the LCC as part of the Festival of Britain Architectural Exhibition. Seven-year-old Albert Snoddy solemnly holds his tortoise, Tommy, while on his right is his sister Jean. The family were presented the keys to the flat by the Mayor and Mayoress of Poplar, Cllr and Mrs G.H. Wells.

View of Tower Bridge, 1950, with Irongate Wharf in the foreground, the General Steam Navigation Company offices on the right, and St Katharine's Dock in the background. Tower Bridge was opened on 30 June 1894. It was designed by Sir Horace Jones, who died before the foundations of the bridge were completed, and the work had to be finished by George Stevenson.

Bing Sings at the Troxy, 1950. The banner on the side of the van advertises Bing Crosby and Nancy Olson in *Mr Music* and is billed for the week commencing 26 December.

Advertising *Peter Pan* in front of John Scurr House, 1950s. The Troxy had an imaginative way of advertising their programmes, using performers dressed for the part touring the streets to drum up trade. They even had a 'Red Indian' on a horse trotting up and down Commercial Road advertising *Two Flags West*. John Scurr House, completed in 1933, was named after one of Poplar's best-known councillors.

Outing to Southend-on-Sea, 2 June 1949. The trip was organised by the Bethnal Green Old People's Welfare Committee, and eight coaches were needed for over 200 old age pensioners who made the trip. Mr Percy Holman, MP for Bethnal Green, is seen in the centre of the group.

Waving goodbye to a group of old age pensioners from Bethnal Green who are off on a day trip to Southend-on-Sea, 19 September 1950.

Spratts (Patent) Ltd, manufacturers of animal foods, in the Coronation Carnival procession, 6 June 1953. Spratts was one of the best-known factories in Poplar.

Hitchmans Dairy supplied this original entry in the Coronation Carnival procession and had quite a following from some of the younger spectators.

Guests leaving the MV *Royal Sovereign* on arrival at Poplar Dock for the official opening of Charrington, Gardner, Locket & Co.'s new fuel oil terminal at Blackwall, 15 September 1958.

Old-time dancing at the bandstand in Victoria Park, 1957. The bandstand was constructed in 1939, but the official opening was cancelled with the onset of war. Throughout the war, jazz concerts, band performances and concert parties were held here, and were very popular. Twice-weekly Modern and Old-time dance evenings were held right up to the summer of 1985.

A courtyard in Grosvenor Buildings, Manisty Street, Poplar, 1950. It must have been a fine day, judging from the curtains drying on the line!

The old wash-houses in Betts Street, St Georges in the East. Mrs Ballard, supervisor at the wash-houses in the early 1960s, chats to Mrs Webbs who is checking her washing on one of the giant pull-out clothes-horses used for drying laundry.

Laying the foundation stone at Reynolds House, April 1951. The rebuilding of the East End continues unabated.

Clearing up the debris at Burns House, June 1955. Demolition is in progress at Bethnal Green to make way for the extension of Bethnal Green Gardens. This view looks north-east of Burns House, Cornwall Avenue. On the right is Shelley House.

The lifeboat belonging to Dockland Settlement enters Millwall Docks, April 1960. The lifeboat was presented to the Settlement by R.G. Odell Ltd, the river bus proprietors and was named *Christie* after Lady Simon, wife of Lord Simon, Chairman of the Port of London Authority.

Snooker at the Brady Boys Club, *c.* 1960. This club for Jewish boys was founded in Brady Street over 100 years ago. A serious game is in progress!

Regents Canal Dock, Limehouse Basin, November 1949. The last of Limehouse – with St Anne's Church in the distance. It takes about half an hour to get the *Grebe* out of the dock in to the Thames, for its run to Rotterdam.

The Making of Tower Hamlets

Bernard Bresslaw (1934–93) at the Mobile Unit, Odeon cinema, Mile End Road, November 1960. Bresslaw came along to endorse the mass X-ray campaign organised by Stepney Borough Council. The actor was born in Stepney, lived in Eric Street and attended the Cooper's School in Bow.

Cllr Mrs Nellie Cressall, Freeman of the Borough, is presented to the Queen and Prince Philip during their visit to Poplar, Wednesday 15 March 1961. Nellie Cressall was a suffragette who fought alongside Sylvia Pankhurst for women's right to vote. As a councillor in Poplar, she was one of the five women who went to jail during the Poplar Rates Dispute in 1921, but was released after 16 days when it was discovered that she was seven months pregnant.

Miss Muriel Lester of Kingsley Hall, Bow and the Mayor of Poplar Cllr J. Gillender JP at Miss Lester's 80th birthday party, 9 December 1963. Muriel and her sister Doris Lester founded Kingsley Hall in Bromley-by-Bow shortly after the First World War. Muriel Lester travelled the world for the Fellowship of Reconciliation, whose aim was peace among nations, and she was a close friend of Mahatma Gandhi.

Fashion Show at Brady Girls Club, 1965. A few of the girls compare fashion notes before the contest. Thirty girls took part in the fashion competition, with the top four going on to the Jewish youth finals. Winners were Janice Lipman, Zippy Groner, Sharon Brewer and Irene Harris.

West India Docks, 1965. Boats and barges line the entrance to the docks, while ships of all sizes and description lie at anchor.

Inspecting ivory at the PLA warehouse in St Katharine's Dock, *c.* 1950. Up to 10,000 elephant tusks, some of them up to 200 lb in weight, would be stored here, and London was the centre of the world's supply of ivory.

Sherry at London Docks, 1961. Part of a shipment of sherry, representing over 600,000 bottles, is shown here being sorted prior to customs examination at London Dock. Two-thirds of the wine and spirits imported into the United Kingdom passed through the Port of London each year.

London Docks, *c.* 1969. The jetty in the background is the Western Dock, with Gordon House and the spire of St Paul's Shadwell just visible in the far distance.

Miriam Moses OBE JP, 1965. Born in Princelet Street, the daughter of Mark Moses, master tailor, Miriam Moses went on to a career in local government and politics, becoming the first woman mayor of Stepney and the first Jewish woman to be elected to that office in England. She helped to found the Brady Girls Club in Hanbury Street, and was the warden there for many years. She died in 1965.

Queen Elizabeth and the Mayor of Stepney Miss E. Aylward at Trinity Almshouses, July 1962. The almshouses were erected in 1625 for '28 decayed masters and commanders of ships or the widows of such'. In 1895 a plan was put forward to demolish the buildings but a campaign headed by C.R. Ashbee, who proposed a counter-plan to refurbish and restore them, was successful. The buildings were badly damaged during the Second World War, and subsequently restored by the LCC.

Tenants of Greencoat Properties Ltd organise a protest march, 26 February 1962. The tenants gathered in Cornfield Street and marched to the home of the company chairman, Lord Broughshaw, in Eaton Square, only to find the house empty. From the 1940s onwards there was a series of protests and rent strikes launched against landlords whom many felt were charging exorbitant rents for decaying flats and houses, which were poorly maintained and seldom repaired.

Three Mills Distillery, *c.* 1969. The three mills on the River Lea have a history of brewing going back centuries. They now consist of the House Mill and the Clock Mill, the third mill having been demolished in Tudor times. In the eighteenth century the mills were owned by Daniel Bisson. These tide mills are the last remaining in the London area and there are only two remaining elsewhere in Britain. After falling into disrepair, the buildings were refurbished in the 1990s and are now managed as a heritage site.

Brady Street dwellings, November 1961. Built by the 4 Per Cent Industrial Dwellings Co. Ltd in 1889–90, the buildings were designed by architect Nathan S. Joseph. They were demolished in 1979.

Ravenscroft Buildings, Bethnal Green, *c*. 1965. The buildings show signs of advanced decay.

Cranbrook Estate, *c.* 1969. The three distinctive tower blocks dominate the horizon. In the foreground can be seen the statue of the Blind Beggar and his Dog, by sculptor Elizabeth Frink.

Wolf Mankowitz, *c.* 1965. Born on 7 November 1924 in Fashion Street, the son of Russian Jews who had come to the East End before the First World War, Wolf Mankowitz became in turn an antiques dealer, novelist, playwright and film and television scriptwriter and director. Among his many successes was *Expresso Bongo, The Day the Earth Caught Fire* and *A Kid for Two Farthings*. He died in June 1998.

Terence Stamp, 1965. Terence was born in the maternity wing of the Mile End Hospital, Bancroft Road, the eldest child of Thomas and Ethel Stamp of Canal Road, Stepney. After training at drama school he worked in repertory, and was noticed by Peter Ustinov while performing in a play *Why the Chicken*, and chosen to play the part of Billy Budd. He was awarded the title of Best Actor of the Year at the 1965 Cannes Film Festival.

Decline and Regeneration

Prospective tenants queuing for flats, 16 January 1976. The GLC announced that they were allotting 120 flats to people on a first-come, first-served basis. To qualify, people must have lived in London for at least a year, and be employed in London. These were considered hard-to-let flats and were only for single people or couples without children. Many of the flats were in need of repair and redecoration. However, they were snapped up within hours, leaving many people disgruntled at not having been 'in the know'.

Asians march in protest against racial violence in the East End, 12 June 1976. After a meeting in the Naz cinema, Brick Lane, where speakers, including the Bishop of Stepney, the Rt Revd Trevor Huddleston, described the sudden and dramatic increase in racial violence in the area, more than 2,000 people marched to Leman Street police station to hand in a letter protesting about the lack of police protection for victims of racial violence.

Whitechapel Bell Foundry, 1976. This bicentennial bell was cast at the Whitechapel Bell Foundry to commemorate the 200th anniversary of the US Declaration of Independence. The inscription cast in relief on the waist of the bell reads: 'For the People of the United States of America from the People of Britain 4th July 1976. Let Freedom Ring.' The bell was installed in a tower at the Independence National Historic Park in Philadelphia in June of that year.

Whitechapel Bell Foundry, 1976. Two workers are busy at a crucial stage in the process of casting. They are seen here tapping the furnace to pour the molten metal from the crucible into a small bell mould.

Arnold Circus and the bandstand which forms the focal point of the Boundary Estate, 1975. In the 1890s a notorious slum called the Old Nichol was demolished and the Boundary Estate built to replace it. The bandstand was constructed in 1910, and a brass band would play here during the summer evenings (see p. 23).

Anglia House on the Walter Edwards Estate, 1970. A view from the south-west showing the newly completed 17-storey block of 66 flats, built on the site of the former Salmon Buildings. In the foreground can be seen the two blocks of 4-storey family maisonnettes, Caledonia and Cambria Houses.

Hackworth Point, Crossways, March 1977. This is one of three tower blocks in Rainhill Way, Bromley-by-Bow. By the 1970s Tower Hamlets had nearly 100 tower blocks, the greatest number over 8 storeys in the whole of London. Hackworth Point, with its 24 storeys, was one of several tower blocks branded by Tony Judge, chairman of the Council's Housing Management Committee, as 'our biggest postwar housing blunder', and suggestions were even put forward that they should be demolished.

Watts Street buildings, 4 April 1977. The problems of poor housing and boarded-up buildings had reached crisis point in Tower Hamlets, which by this time was being accused of having the worst record for housing in the whole of London.

Bakery in Quaker Street, Spitalfields, 1978. The baker weighs the dough after kneading, dividing it into individual loaves ready for the final proving. Independent small bakers were soon to be priced out of business by the supermarkets, although some held on stubbornly into the 1980s.

Bloom's Kosher Restaurant, Whitechapel High Street, 1978. Customers queue at the counter waiting to be served. Bloom's was world-famous as an authentic Jewish restaurant, and with its closure following a visit by the Jewish inspector the East End lost one of its last links with its Jewish traditions.

The Prime Minister James Callaghan and Peter Shore MP touring the docks, 1976. In February 1976 there was a massive campaign to save the West India and Millwall Docks from closure. The Port of London Authority was planning to close the docks and transfer their activities to the Royal Docks. However, many dockers at the time feared that eventually the Royal Docks would share the same fate. Docklands MPs and delegations from the unions met the chairman of the PLA Board, who assured them that this was not the case. Within the next ten years, all the docks in the East End of London were closed.

Queen Elizabeth visiting St Katharine's, 9 June 1977. The Mayor of Tower Hamlets, Cllr Riley in attendance. The royal visit was part of the Silver Jubilee River Progress.

Petticoat Lane Market, Middlesex Street, Whitechapel, 1975. Going down the lane was still as popular in the 1970s as it had been at the turn of the century, and today the market has spilled over into surrounding streets and is a major tourist attraction.

Davis Mansions playground, Spitalfields Project, 1978. Improving the neighbourhoods to make them safer for children to play in was just one of the schemes launched by the Spitalfields Project, a major initiative to improve the area.

French polisher at East London Furniture Company, 1981. Cabinet-making was once an important trade in the East End, especially in Shoreditch and Curtain Road, but factory-produced goods have turned a skill into a dying art.

Englefields Ltd, 1980. The foreman Mr Topper pours out the molten metal.

Princess Alexandra opens the new road scheme on the Isle of Dogs, September 1983. The Red Brick Road was a great innovation at the time, and signalled the beginning of the regeneration of the docklands area.

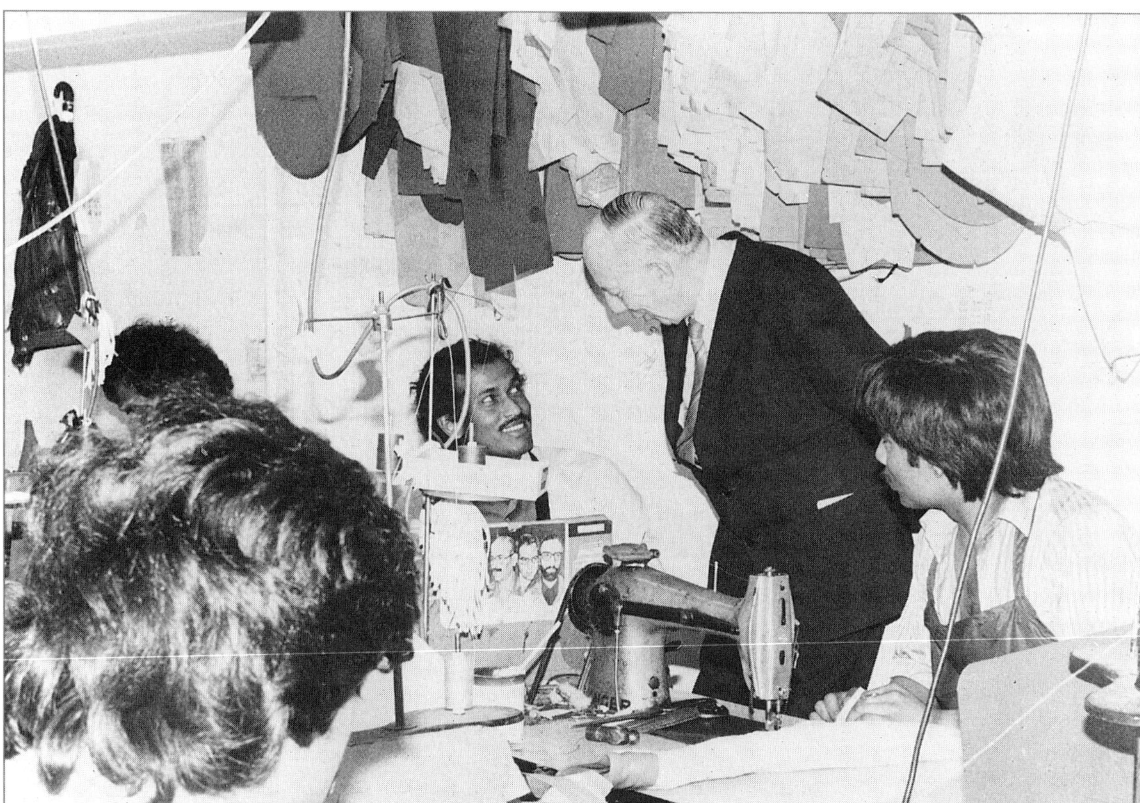

Tailoring workshop in Brick Lane, 1984. Donald Chesworth, warden of Toynbee Hall, talks to garment workers. Whitechapel has been the centre of the rag trade in London for over 150 years, and where sweat shops could be found in rooms and attics in every street and alley, the trade is now better regulated and organised.

Towards the Millennium

Barbara Windsor opening the new cinema Genesis in the Mile End Road, June 1999. Seen with the famous East End actress is the proprietor, Tyrone Walker-Hebborn, and his parents. In 1912 the Paragon Theatre of Varieties was converted into a cinema, and renamed the Mile End Empire. It became the ABC in 1934, and in 1963 the premiere of *Sparrows Can't Sing* starring Barbara Windsor was held at the ABC in the presence of Lord Snowdon. It was called the Coronet when it finally closed its doors in 1989. Now as Genesis the cinema will provide entertainment for yet another generation of East Enders.

The Jamme Masjid, the Great Mosque on the corner of Fournier Street and Brick Lane, 1997. The building was originally constructed in 1743 as a Huguenot chapel, which became a Methodist chapel and was then converted into a synagogue, the Machzik Hadass. With the decline in the Jewish population the synagogue was abandoned until the building was restored and refurbished in 1975 to house the Jamme Masjid, for the Moslem community.

The East London Mosque in Whitechapel Road, 1997. The mosque was built in 1985 as a place of worship for the growing Moslem community in the Whitechapel area.

Results of the great storm of 16 October 1987. Trees uprooted in St Dunstan's churchyard are being cleared away by volunteers. St Dunstan's parish church dates back to Saxon times, and is situated in what was once the village of Stepney, facing Stepney Green.

Prince Charles tries his hand at bricklaying, September 1988. The Prince launched the Rosehaugh self-build scheme in Dunbridge Street, Bethnal Green.

West India Dock Road, November 1990. The view is towards the south-east, and the West India Docks. In the distance is Charlie Brown's Railway Tavern, and the building on the extreme right was the Chinese Mission. In between were Chinese restaurants and shops. All this was to disappear with the widening of the West India Dock Road and the construction of the Limehouse Link.

Gurdwara in Harley Grove, 1991. Originally built as a Congregational chapel, in September 1927 it was converted into a synagogue for the Jewish community, but faced with a dwindling congregation, the synagogue held its final service in April 1977. After falling into disuse, it was taken over by the local Sikh community as their place of worship.

Diana, Princess of Wales, in conversation with staff at the Globe Town Neighbourhood Centre, 62 Roman Road, 16 January 1990. The visit was to mark the first anniversary of an arrangement between Outset Office Services and Globe Town to employ a certain number of disabled people in their offices.

Children take a ride in a horse caravan on the occasion of the unveiling of a plaque to the East London Suffragettes on the site of the Women's Hall, 400 Old Ford Road, Bow, 1993. The plaque was unveiled by Mrs Caroline Benn, wife of Tony Benn MP.

Statue of Clement Attlee outside Limehouse Library, Commercial Road, 1991. Attlee was a councillor in Stepney, Mayor of Stepney in 1920 and was elected MP for Limehouse in 1922.

Rachel Whiteread's prize-winning sculpture, 'House' in Grove Road, Bow. The sculpture is the cast of the inside of a house, formerly 193 Grove Road, once the home of the Gale family. The sculpture won the Turner Prize in November 1993 with a cash prize of £60,000. It was demolished in January 1994. Local reaction can be judged by the graffiti on the side: 'Wot For'.

Whitehorse Workshop, March 1985. Passing on traditional skills of the craftsman to the next generation.

Painting and Decorating, April 1993. Work experience pilot project – trainees from Community Industry, Palmers Road, decorating pensioners' homes on the Osier, Longnor and Norfolk estates.

Rikki Shields, an Australian Aborigine in Meath Gardens, 31 July 1996. King Cole, Australian Aborigine cricketer, was a member of the first Australian cricket team to tour England. It was composed entirely of Aborigines. He died of tuberculosis in Guys Hospital, London on 24 June 1868 and was buried in Victoria Park cemetery, now Meath Gardens. In 1988 a plaque was placed in Meath Gardens, and a eucalyptus tree was planted in his memory. The plaque was later stolen, but in 1996 a new plaque was unveiled by the Australian Deputy High Commissioner, and Rikki Shields, who lives in London, performed a moving ceremony, placing sacred objects around the plaque which, he explained, would help the bones and spirit of King Cole on the journey to its beginning time.

The Bishop of Stepney the Rt Revd Richard Chartres, and the Mayor Cllr Kofi Appiah unveil a plaque marking the 50th anniversary of the Bethnal Green Tube Disaster, 3 March 1993. Before the unveiling ceremony, a memorial service was held in St John's Church, Cambridge Heath Road, opposite the tube station.

Spitalfields Market, 1997. Built in 1928 on the site of a medieval market, the Spitalfields fruit and vegetable market moved to Temple Mills in 1987, when it was found that container lorries had difficulty in negotiating the narrow streets. A plan to turn the building into a financial centre for London has been dropped and the market is now home to a variety of arts and crafts stalls, vegetarian and whole food shops and is still expanding.

Banglatown archway in Brick Lane, 1997. The area was renamed Banglatown to reflect the large Bangladeshi community who now reside and trade in the Brick Lane area.

A view of Billingsgate Market, with Canary Wharf in the background. The world-famous fish market, which is run by the Corporation of London, was moved into a new Docklands site from its traditional centuries-old site in Lower Thames Street and opened for business on 19 January 1982.

The Canary Wharf complex with NATO warships in the foreground, 1991.

Acknowledgements and Picture Credits

Associated Press Ltd
Boxing News
Nicholas Breach
British Council
British Museum
Central News
Central Press Photos
Crafts
J. Connor
John Cowan
Daily Herald
Daily Mail
East London Advertiser
Federation of Synagogues
Fox Photos
Halifax Photos Ltd
IISG (International Institute for Social History, Amsterdam)
Mr Ivory
John Topham Picture Library
Keystone Press Agency
London Metropolitan Archives
H.J. Malby
New York Times
Pettingal
Philip Mernick
Photopress
Poplar Methodist Mission
Port of London Authority
David Rich
K.R. Royden
Sport & General Press Agency
Sealand Aerial Photography
Stepney Jewish Club
R.F. Taylor
The *Graphic*
E.W. Tottersall
Tower Hamlets Local History Library and Archives
Mr W. Turner
Tyrone Walker-Hebborn (Genesis Ltd)
William Whiffin Collection
Whitechapel Mission